DATE DUE

Twenty
Names In
AVIATION

Jason Hook

Illustrated by Graham Coton

MARSHALL CAVENDISH
New York · London · Toronto · Sydney

Editor: Sophie Davies
Consultant Editor: Maggi McCormick

Reference Edition published 1990

© Marshall Cavendish Limited 1990
© Wayland (Publishers) Limited 1989

Published by Marshall Cavendish Corporation
147, West Merrick Road
Freeport
Long Island
N.Y. 11520

Library of Congress Cataloging-in-Publication Data

Hook, Jason
   Twenty names in aviation / Jason Hook : illustrated by Graham Coton.
      p. cm. – (Twenty names)
   Includes bibliographical references.
   Summary: Brief biographies of twenty aviation pioneers from the
Montgolfier brothers to Bryan Allen and his human powered airplane.
   ISBN 1-85435-253-9
   1. Aeronautics – Biography – Juvenile literature. [1. Aeronautics -
Biography.] I. Coton, Graham. ill. II. Title. III. Title: 20 names in
aviation. IV. Series.
TL539.H62 1989
629.13'092'2-dc20
[B]   89-23912
[920]   CIP
                                                            AC

Printed in Italy by G. Canale & C. S.p.A., Turin.

Contents

The Story of Aviation

Throughout the ages, people have looked with envy to the skies and longed to take flight like the birds.

The great aviation parable is the 3,000-year-old Greek myth of Icarus. Imprisoned on the island of Crete by King Minos, he escaped, with his father Daedalus, on wings of wax and feathers. Excited by the thrill of flying, Icarus soared too close to the sun. The wax in his wings melted, and he plunged to his death in the sea below.

Throughout history, would-be aviators have leaped from towers, flapping wings of leather, cloth, wood and feathers. Many plunged like Icarus to their deaths. In the fifteenth century, the artistic and scientific genius Leonardo da Vinci made detailed studies of bird flight and illustrated designs for a helicopter and a parachute. He too, though, was obsessed with designing an aircraft with flapping wings (an ornithopter). Unfortunately, human muscles were simply incapable of powering such a machine.

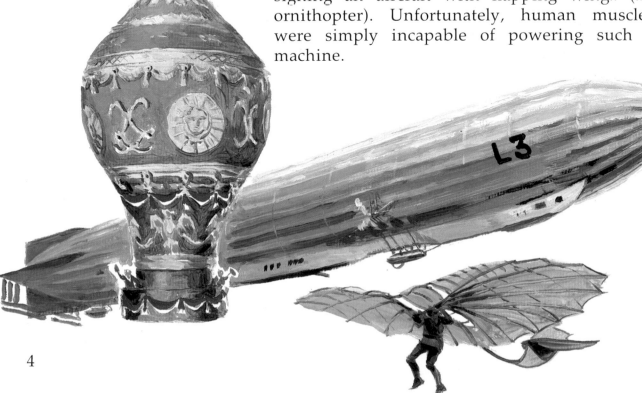

The ancient dream of flight was eventually achieved in lighter-than-air craft, through the balloons of two French brothers, the Montgolfiers. Not until this century did the Wright brothers begin the modern age of heavier-than-air powered aviation. Since then, the short history of the airplane has been one of extraordinary progress, achieved through the work of courageous pioneers like those in this book. From Louis Blériot's first crossing of the English Channel, through the solo transatlantic flights of Charles Lindbergh and Amelia Earhart, to the supersonic age heralded by Chuck Yeager, the fledgling airplane had matured into a beast of great power.

The development of flight is perhaps the supreme achievement of our age.

1
The Montgolfier Brothers

Sitting at home in front of the fire one evening, Joseph Montgolfier, a papermaker from Annonay in France, grew fascinated by the sparks rushing up the chimney. He made a bag from silk rags and held it over the fire. He then released it, watching with satisfaction as the simple hot-air balloon fluttered up to the ceiling.

Assisted by his brother Etienne, Joseph began sending huge smoke-filled balloons soaring into the sky. Word reached King Louis XVI, and on September 19, 1783, the brothers gave a command performance of their discovery at the Court of Versailles. An excited crowd of thousands watched as a sheep, duck and rooster were carried upward in a wicker basket hanging below the beautifully decorated Montgolfière balloon. They landed safely in a wood two miles away, becoming the first living creatures to be carried into the air in a balloon.

1740 Joseph-Michel Montgolfier born in Annonay, France
1745 Jacques-Etienne Montgolfier born
1782 Joseph discovers the hot-air balloon
1783 the first public balloon flight; (Sept.) living creatures fly in a balloon for the first time; (Nov.) people fly in a balloon for the first time
1784 Joseph makes his only flight
1799 Etienne dies traveling from Lyons to Annonay
1810 Joseph dies at Balaruc-les-Bains

Right *A great crowd gathered to see the Montgolfier brothers' balloon carry a sheep, a duck and a rooster high over Versailles, near Paris.*

The brothers began constructing a balloon large enough to carry a person up into the clouds. King Louis offered two condemned criminals to try this dangerous experiment, but a young historian, Jean-Francois Pilatre de Rozier, insisted that he should claim the honor of the first human flight. On November 21, 1783, Rozier, accompanied by the Marquis d'Arlandes, climbed into a gallery under the balloon. Stoking a blazing iron brazier slung below them and frantically putting out the flying sparks that threatened to destroy the balloon's linen canopy, the two men rose steadily above an astonished crowd gathered at a Paris chateau. For twenty-five minutes the great *Montgolfière* carried the world's first balloonists high over Paris.

Ballooning soon became the great craze of Europe, where the Montgolfier brothers became very famous. Through their discovery of a "cloud enclosed in a bag," people had at last risen up into the sky.

The brothers launch a huge balloon at Jardin Reveillon, near Paris.

2
George Cayley

During his life, George Cayley, a baronet from Yorkshire in England, applied his inventive mind to subjects as diverse as unemployment and artificial human limbs. He was a philosopher, a Member of Parliament and a brilliant pioneer in the field of aviation.

At the age of ten, Cayley was inspired by the Montgolfiers' balloon flights, but like many great men before him, he yearned to fly more like the birds. Through his extraordinary efforts to accomplish this feat with navigable, heavier-than-air machines, Cayley became known as the "father of the airplane."

In 1799, Cayley, aged twenty-six, engraved on a silver disk the first known design for a fixed-wing airplane. Except for having paddles instead of a propeller, it included all the features of a modern aircraft. Most importantly, Cayley's airplane had fixed wings to lift it into the air, rather than the flapping wings that previous inventors had used to provide power.

Right *Cayley's coachman reluctantly made the world's first gliding flight over a valley at Brompton Hall in England.*

Having studied bird flight, Cayley constructed a kite-shaped model glider, the world's first true airplane. Within five years he was flying, unmanned, a full-sized glider. He had also published papers: "On Aerial Navigation," containing all the principles of heavier-than-air flight.

After various studies, Cayley returned in his later years to building gliders, briefly sending a ten-year-old boy up in a triplane. Four years before his death, Cayley launched his aged coachman unsteadily over a small valley, in the first manned gliding flight in history.

Cayley kept heavier-than-air flight alive at a time when it was ridiculed. He predicted that: "Aerial navigation will form a most prominent feature in the process of civilization." His enthusiasm, though, was not shared by his coachman. When Cayley approached him, tears of joy glistening in his eyes after the historic flight, the trembling pilot declared: "Please, Sir George, I wish to give notice. I was hired to drive, not to fly."

1773	born at Brompton Hall, Scarborough, England
1799	designs the first modern airplane
1804	builds the first true airplane
1809	publishes "On Aerial Navigation"
1843	designs a "convertiplane," combining the helicopter and the world's first biplane
1849	sends a small boy up in a glider
1853	his coachman achieves first ever gliding flight
1857	dies, aged eighty-four, at Brompton Hall

3
Count von Zeppelin

In 1884, *La France*, the world's first successful "dirigible" – a navigable airship – made its maiden voyage. The publicity caught the attention of a lieutenant general in the German cavalry, Count Ferdinand von Zeppelin, who quickly realized that the airship could have military uses.

Zeppelin had been an army officer since the age of nineteen. He had made his only flight in a balloon on a military mission in Minnesota. Some years later, he studied the possibility of a huge airship made with gas balloons inside a rigid covered framework.

At the age of fifty-two, Zeppelin was retired in disgrace from the cavalry after becoming involved in a political matter. He turned his mind to airships, and ten years later launched *Zeppelin No. 1*. The Count flew this 415 foot (128 m) long cigar-shaped monster for twenty minutes, but its performance was disappointing. Zeppelin's personal fortune was nearly spent, and only funds from a state lottery allowed him to continue his work.

1838 born in Konstanz, Germany
1870 begins studying giant airships
1900 *LZ 1* makes her first flight
1907 *LZ 3* creates airship flight duration record
1910–14 Delag flies the first passenger airline
1915–18 Zeppelins bomb Britain
1917 dies at Charlottenburg, Germany
1929 *Graf Zeppelin* flies around the world
1937 *Hindenburg* explodes at Lakehurst, N.J.

When *Zeppelin No. 2* was destroyed by storms, the courageous Count immediately began on his third airship. *LZ 3* broke all records by remaining airborne for eight hours, and Zeppelin, ridiculed until then, became a national hero.

Zeppelin formed his airships into the world's first passenger airline, Delag, which carried 35,000 passengers between Germany's cities, without injury, before World War I. In 1914, the great Zeppelins became weapons of war and flew over Britain in terrifying bombing raids.

After Zeppelin's death, his airships continued to make headlines. In 1929, the magnificent, luxurious *Graf Zeppelin* made the first round-the-world passenger flight. Eight years later, her successor, the *Hindenburg*, burst into flames near Lakehurst, New Jersey. Thirty-five people died, and the age of the airship came to an end.

Above *The Hindenburg explodes while landing at Lakehurst, New Jersey, May 6, 1937.*

Below *Zeppelin airships made frequent bombing raids over Britain during World War I.*

4
Otto Lilienthal

"To design a flying machine is nothing; to build it is not much; to fly it is everything." This belief set the German pioneer Otto Lilienthal apart from the many inventors who, after Cayley's success, attempted to leap from the ground in various wonderful flying machines.

After graduating from Berlin Technical Academy and serving in the Franco-Prussian War (1870–71), Lilienthal became a civil engineer. Throughout his life, he believed that the perfect motion of birds held the secret to flight. As a boy, he strapped wings to his arms and tried to fly. While he was in college, he constructed a six-wing ornithopter. Lilienthal studied bird flight more closely than anyone before him. His 1889 work *Bird Flight as the Basis of Aviation* influenced a whole generation of aviators.

Lilienthal's greatest achievement was his flying of gliders, demonstrating that before applying power to an airplane, people must first master the air. In 1891, in a fixed-wing glider, he flew for the first time. In the next five years, Lilienthal flew his gliders from the housetops of Berlin and the Rhinower Hills in over 2,000 successful flights. He learned to steer his gliders. On one flight, he even made a turn of 180 degrees, to end up facing in the opposite direction.

1848 born at Anklam, Germany
1867–70 studies at Berlin Technical Academy
1869 builds an ornithopter
1870 serves in Franco-Prussian War
1889 publishes *Bird Flight as the Basis Of Aviation*
1891–96 makes over 2,000 glider flights
1896 crashes in the Rhinower Hills and dies the next day in the Bergmann Clinic, Berlin

Right *Lilienthal mastered the art of gliding in the Rhinower Hills near Berlin.*

Developments in photography meant that many people saw pictures of Lilienthal soaring through the air, hanging by his arms from his glider's beautiful wings made of willow wands and cotton cloth. Few could now doubt the human ability to fly.

Tragically, Lilienthal was thinking of attempting powered flight when he crashed one of his gliders and broke his back. He was the world's first true aviator, and his gravestone bears the words: "Sacrifices must be made."

Above *One of the Lilienthal's elegant gliders, preserved at the British Science Museum, London.*

5

The Wright Brothers

On December 17, 1903, Orville Wright, watched by his brother Wilbur, guided their *Flyer* biplane unsteadily into the air. For the next twelve seconds he flew over the Kill Devil sand dunes, landing safely to complete the world's first piloted, sustained flight in a powered airplane: the greatest landmark in aviation history.

Lilienthal's gliding photographs had first inspired the Wrights' interest in flying, while their bicycle manufacturing business provided funds and a workshop. Following early experiments with a biplane kite and gliders, they built a wind tunnel to conduct detailed research. The results enabled them to make nearly a thousand successful gliding flights near Kitty Hawk, North Carolina. Their dream, however, was to achieve powered flight.

Their first powered airplane, *Flyer*, with an engine and propeller of their own design, achieved a best flight of fifty-nine seconds on that historic December day. By 1905, Wilbur had

1867 Wilbur born in Millville, Indiana
1871 Orville born in Dayton, Ohio
1899 their first aircraft, a biplane kite, flies
1903 world's first powered airplane flight
1905 Wilbur flies 25 miles (39km)
1908 Wilbur's flights amaze Europe; Orville's passenger killed
1909 Wrights tour Europe and the U.S.
1912 Wilbur dies in Dayton
1948 Orville dies in Dayton

Right *In 1903, Orville Wright made the world's first real airplane flight.*

14

made a flight of nearly 25 miles (39km) in *Flyer III*, the world's first practical airplane. Remarkably, the world ignored these achievements. For three years the brothers gave up flying.

Then Wilbur toured Europe, first demonstrating his airplane's excellence at a race in France. A critical audience was stunned by his masterful flying. The Wright brothers' accomplishments were at last recognized. Orville, meanwhile, secured U.S. Army interest in the *Flyer*, despite a crash in which he was seriously injured and his passenger was killed.

The Wright brothers toured Rome, Paris and London. Their acclaimed flights stimulated the great European air age. They returned triumphantly to the United States, giving demonstrations, training pilots and receiving many honors for their historic achievements.

Wilbur spent his last years defending the patents that protected their inventions. His early death from typhoid fever devastated Orville, who continued his aviation work in the airplane age, which he and his brother had created.

Orville guides the Flyer *over the sand dunes near Kitty Hawk, North Carolina.*

6

Louis Blériot

Before the Wrights taught the world to fly, many European pioneers risked their lives in the race to achieve powered flight. Lacking suitable theory, they attempted to fly through the sheer force of engine and propeller.

Typical of this era was Louis Blériot, a dashing Frenchman who financed his aviation exploits with a fortune made from manufacturing automobile headlights. He first flew in gliders towed along the River Seine. Then he tried unsuccessfully to fly biplanes. Finally, he turned to building monoplanes and became a leading aviation pioneer.

In 1907, he made several short aerial hops in his *Blériot VI* monoplane, before crashing twice and nearly killing himself. His next machine, which closely resembled a modern light airplane, was abandoned after another accident. It was only after witnessing Wilbur Wright's celebrated European flights that Blériot was able to produce his successful *XI* monoplane.

1872 born in Cambrai, France
1907 *Blériot VI* makes hop-flights
1909 flies the English Channel
1909 dominates first Reims meeting
1909 makes first flight in Rumania
1912 Harriet Quimby becomes first woman to fly the Channel in a Blériot monoplane
1936 dies in Paris

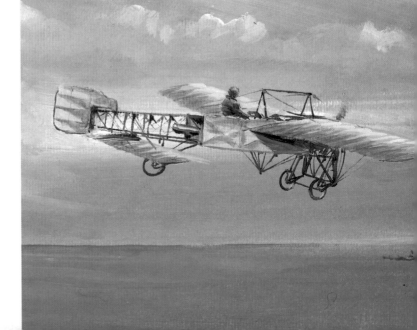

When the British *Daily Mail* newspaper offered £1,000 to the first aviator to cross the English Channel, a race developed between Blériot and an Englishman, Hubert Latham. After Latham's unsuccessful first attempt, the two men awaited good weather on the French cost. At 4 a.m. on July 25, 1909, Blériot climbed into his monoplane. He discarded his crutches – the result of another of his famous accidents – declaring: "I won't want them again until I come back from England." At daybreak, Blériot flew from Les Baraques out over the Channel. Thirty-six minutes later, the courageous Frenchman crash-landed his alarmingly fragile monoplane near Dover Castle on the English coast. The epic flight proved that planes could conquer the seas that divided nations.

Blériot gained lasting fame. Orders poured in for the *XI* monoplane. He dominated the first great aviation meeting held at Reims in France and flew throughout Europe, crashing again in Turkey. During World War I (1914–18), he built aircraft for France before turning to commercial airplane development.

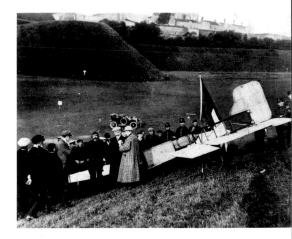

Above *Blériot (in flying suit) strikes a typical pose after his historic Channel flight.*

Below *Blériot approaches Dover castle and the end of the first cross-channel flight.*

7
Alberto Santos-Dumont

"For us aviators, your name is a banner. You are our Pathfinder." So Louis Blériot described Alberto Santos-Dumont, a dynamic Brazilian whose achievements and powerful personality inspired Europe's aviation pioneers.

During his childhood, Alberto drove steam engines on his father's coffee plantation and found inspiration in Jules Verne's fantasy novels. He traveled to Paris to study when his father's death made him a very wealthy man.

After making a balloon flight in Paris, Santos-Dumont built a navigable airship (a dirigible) powered by a gasoline engine, from which grew a fleet of airships. He often sailed over the Paris rooftops, tethering his airship outside his favorite coffee house or crashing spectacularly into the treetops. His most famous flight, circling the Eiffel Tower from the suburb of St. Cloud, won

him the 100,000 franc Henri Deutsch prize.

Visiting the U.S., Santos-Dumont learned of the Wrights' early achievements. He returned to France and constructed his first airplane, the *14-bis*, which was tested suspended from his *No. 14* airship. It was a huge, ungainly machine, with its tail at the front, propeller at the rear, and great box kite wings. Yet, Santos-Dumont forced it clumsily into the air. His astonishing 725 foot (220m) flight in 1906 – the first such flight in Europe – won him enormous acclaim.

Santos-Dumont's final achievement was his famous *Demoiselle*, the world's first successful light airplane, with a wingspan of only 18 feet (5.5m) and a top speed of 60mph (96.5kph). A year after its production, illness forced him to retire. After a slow decline, Santos-Dumont returned to Brazil. He became very depressed about the use of aircraft for warfare. In 1932, he committed suicide.

1870	born in Minas Gerais, Brazil
1898	builds his first airship
1901	circles Eiffel Tower in *No. 6* airship
1906	builds his first airplane; wins Arohdoacon prize for a 198 foot (60m) flight; flies 725 feet (220m) in 21.2 seconds
1909	produces *Demoiselle* airplane
1910	retires
1928	returns to Brazil to a hero's welcome
1932	dies in São Paulo, Brazil

Santos-Dumont won the acclaim of Europe when he circled the Eiffel Tower in his No. 6 *airship.*

8
John Alcock and Arthur Whitten Brown

"It is impossible." Such was the official view of a non-stop Atlantic crossing when Alcock and Brown flew from Newfoundland, Canada, on June 14, 1919, aiming for Britain.

Captain John Alcock and Lieutenant Arthur Whitten Brown were both trained engineers. They had been shot down and imprisoned in Turkey when flying for Britain in World War I. Alcock's many piloting exploits included the bombing of Constantinople, while Brown had studied navigation during his imprisonment.

After the war, Alcock became a test pilot for Vickers Aircraft as they prepared an airplane to challenge for a £10,000 British newspaper prize for the first non-stop Atlantic crossing. Brown was recruited as his navigator. Their Vickers Vimy bomber was shipped to St. Johns, Newfoundland.

The biplane bomber, weighed down by 870 gallons (3,293 liters) of fuel, lurched reluctantly

1886	Arthur Whitten Brown born in Glasgow, Scotland, to American parents
1892	John William Alcock born in Manchester, England
1919	first non-stop crossing of the Atlantic, coast to coast time of 15 hours 57 mintues. Alcock crashes near Rouen, France. Dies in Cottévrard, France
1948	Brown dies in Swansea, Wales

Right *Brown balanced on the wing, cleaning the gauges, as the bomber droned on over the Atlantic.*

into the air from Lester's Field. Fog covered the Atlantic, eventually becoming so thick that Alcock, unable to see his wingtips, lost all sense of balance. The bomber nose-dived, looping less than 500 feet (150 m) above the waves before swooping back on course. Then bad weather battered the airplane, and Brown was forced to clamber onto the wing to wipe ice from the gauges.

At last, they sighted Ireland. The bomber landed nose-first in a Galway bog. The two aviators were cheered by huge crowds and were later knighted by King George V. They had achieved the "impossible," crossing the Atlantic in just under sixteen hours.

In the same year, Alcock was tragically killed on a flight to deliver an aircraft to Paris. Brown subsequently returned to engineering with Vickers.

Their historic first transatlantic flight is commemorated by a statue at Heathrow Airport near London. Their airplane can still be seen in the Science Museum in London.

After a flight of 1,961 miles (3,138 km), Alcock and Brown crash-landed in Galway, Ireland.

9
Igor Sikorsky

Igor Sikorsky's mother read to him about Leonardo da Vinci's designs for a helicopter, the flying machine that would eventually make him famous. When he was only twelve years old and still living in Russia, Igor built his first helicopter, a rubber-band-powered model which did fly.

Sikorsky attended St. Petersburg Naval Academy and Kiev Polytechnic, but he preferred solving practical problems in his own workshop. He visited Paris, where he met leading aviation pioneers. He bought a lightweight engine and returned to Russia to construct a full-sized helicopter. Its failure caused him to turn instead to airplane design.

Supported by his family, Sikorsky built and piloted an improving series of airplanes. His work culminated in *Le Grand*, the world's first four-engined aircraft. With a wingspan of 92 feet (28 m), furnished passenger lounge and fully enclosed cabin, it was years ahead of its time, the forerunner of modern airliners.

After the Russian Revolution in 1917, Sikorsky emigrated, with little money, to New York. His English was poor, but he scraped a living lecturing, before founding an aeronautical com-

1889 born in Kiev, Russia
1910 builds "S" series of airplanes
1911 earns International Pilot's Licence No. 64
1913 flies *Le Grand*
1919 emigrates to U.S.
1924 flies *S-29-A*, his first American airplane
1931 produces *S-40* American Clipper
1942 *VS-300* becomes world's first practical helicopter
1957 retires as manager of his engineering company
1972 dies in Easton, Connecticut

Right *Sikorsky's helicopters have played an important part in the development of air-sea rescue.*

pany with other Russian emigrés. They built an excellent airplane from old parts. It re-established Sikorsky's reputation. By the 1930s, he was designing the flying boats which pioneered American transpacific passenger airways.

Equipped with new knowledge and materials, Sikorsky returned to his first love, the helicopter. At the age of fifty, he excitedly piloted his first successful machine in a tethered flight. He soon achieved free flight and set an endurance record. He established his *VS-300* as the world's first fully practical single-rotor helicopter.

The remarkable development of Sikorsky's helicopters and their use today, both in saving lives and at war, bear testimony to an outstanding pioneer, whose career altered the history of powered aviation.

A Sikorsky helicopter in use today in the Belgian Air Force.

10
Manfred von Richthofen

When Manfred Freiherr von Richthofen first fought in World War I, there were no fighter aircraft. Soon, though, pilots were firing machine guns at each other in airborne battles known as "dogfights." Richthofen was to become the most famous "flying ace" of all.

The eldest son of an aristocratic military family, Richthofen graduated from cadet school and became a cavalry officer. Disillusioned with the war on the ground, he transferred to the Air Service. He crashed attempting his first solo flight, but later graduated from Doberitz pilot school to the elite squadron of Oswald Boelcke, Germany's leading ace.

After scoring his first official victory by shooting down a British plane, Richthofen began ordering engraved silver trophies to commemorate each of his "kills." With sixteen victories to his name, he became Germany's greatest living ace and was awarded the coveted *Pour le Mérite* medal. Richthofen became a national hero,

1892 born in Breslau, Germany
1910–11 studies at Berlin War Academy
1915 observer with Air Service
1916 joins Oswald Boelcke's Jasta 2 fighter squadron
1916 scores first victory
1917 awarded Pour le Mérite medal
1917 makes twenty-one kills in "Bloody April"
1917 commands Jagdegeschwader 1
1918 killed over Sailly-de-Sac, France

appearing on souvenir postcards and receiving fan mail. His scarlet-painted airplane earned him the title of the Red Baron.

The silversmith was busy in "Bloody April," 1917, engraving twenty-one trophies for Richthofen, who exceeded fifty victories by shooting down four planes in one day. He became the first commander of the famous Jagdegeschwader 1 air combat group, which, with its multi-colored fighter aircraft, became known as "Richthofen's Flying Circus."

In 1918, pursuing one more "kill," Richthofen was caught between Australian field artillery on the ground and Captain A. R. Brown's RAF Sopwith Camel airplane. He crashed, mortally wounded, and his famous red Fokker aircraft was stripped by souvenir hunters. Perhaps this was fitting, for his own room was filled with his victims' aircraft serial numbers, propellers, machine guns and other trophies. An airplane engine served as a chandelier, while his silver cups commemorated sixty of the eighty kills that made the Red Baron a legend.

The sight of Richthofen's scarlet-painted plane spread terror among the British pilots, who dubbed him the Bloody Red Baron.

11
Charles Kingsford-Smith

Between World Wars I and II, many aviators demonstrated the airplane's potential for long-distance flights. One of the greatest pioneers was an Australian, Charles Kingsford-Smith, whose flights linked countries divided by vast oceans and laid the foundations for today's commercial airways.

Kingsford-Smith always had a passionate love of flying. During World War I, he rose from despatch rider to Royal Flying Corps veteran. Later, when flying demonstrations known as barnstorming shows kept aviation alive, he flew stunts in Hollywood.

Returning to Australia as a civil pilot, Kingsford-Smith dreamed of flying across the immense Pacific Ocean. His dream was fulfilled in 1928 when, with a close friend, Charles Ulm, he flew his *Southern Cross* monoplane 7,430 miles (11,890 km) from Oakland Field, San Francisco, via Hawaii and Fiji, to Brisbane in Australia.

1897 born in Hamilton, Australia
1928 makes the first transpacific flight
1928 makes first return flight over Tasman Sea
1928 forms Australian National Airways
1930 flies the Atlantic
1931 flies Australian airmail to England
1932 knighted by King George V
1933 establishes England–Australia record
1934 makes first Australia–U.S. flight
1935 disappears on the way to Australia

Kingsford-Smith and Ulm crash-land in a swamp after one of their many epic flights together.

Established as a hero in his own country, he made the first return flight over the Tasman Sea linking Australia and New Zealand. Next, he conquered the Atlantic the hard way, from Portmarnock, Ireland, to Newfoundland, Canada, flying "blind" through fog and gales. Traveling to Oakland Field, he became the first aviator to circle the world.

Founding Australian National Airways, the tireless flyer established an Australia-to-England airmail service, making record-breaking flights between the two countries. He was knighted before flying the Pacific again, this time from Australia to the United States.

In 1935, Kingsford-Smith left London for Australia, planning to make the trip his farewell flight. It proved true in a tragic sense. His airplane *Lady Southern Cross* mysteriously disappeared. Wreckage was recovered off Burma two years later.

Kingsford-Smith in the cockpit of the Southern Cross.

12
Amelia Earhart

In 1928, the Fokker seaplane *Friendship* flew from Newfoundland, Canada to Wales. One of its crew members, Amelia Earhart, became the first woman to fly the Atlantic. Although she achieved great fame, she also faced criticism. There were suggestions that she was just a "sack of potatoes" while her male companions did all the flying. In those days, many people did not believe that it was possible for a woman to fly the Atlantic alone.

Earhart, who had learned to fly in college, resolved to do just that. Four years later, she took off from Newfoundland again, this time alone. The long, lonely flight through storms and ice clouds tested all her considerable flying skill, but she landed triumphantly the next day in an Irish meadow. Earhart was the first woman to fly the North Atlantic solo. She was also the only person to make a solo crossing since Charles Lindbergh had flown the same distance in 1927.

1898 born in Atchison, Kansas
1928 becomes the first woman to fly across the Atlantic
1932 first woman's solo flight across the Atlantic
1935 first solo flight from Hawaii to California
1937 disappears near Howland Island, central Pacific, during around-the-world flight

Right *Earhart makes the long, lonely flight over the north Atlantic, achieving the first solo woman's flight.*

Earhart's historic flight and her striking personality earned her a fame that was now undoubtedly deserved. She became the first woman to fly non-stop across the U.S., and she played a leading role in establishing her country's commercial airlines. Realizing the importance of weather forecasting and navigational instruments to aviation, Earhart also predicted the arrival of transpacific airways after making the first solo flight from Hawaii to California. She also founded the "Ninety-nines," the first society of women pilots.

In 1937, Amelia Earhart set out to fly around the world with navigator Fred Noonan. Having completed two-thirds of the flight, she flew from New Guinea out over the South Pacific. Earhart transmitted radio messages, but they were distorted by static. Later, the airplane vanished near Howland Island in the central Pacific. There was much speculation about what happened, but the disappearance of the world's greatest woman aviator remains a complete mystery.

Above *The* Friendship *lands off the coast of Wales, and Amelia Earhart becomes the first woman crew member to cross the Atlantic.*

13
Charles Lindbergh

The pioneering flights of the 1930s were inspired by the most celebrated of all aviators, Charles Lindbergh, the first man to fly the Atlantic solo.

After studying at a flying school, Lindbergh traveled throughout the U.S. as wing-walker, parachutist and stunt flyer with barnstorming tours. Later, he graduated from army flying school and became an airmail pilot, on the St. Louis-Chicago route. Lindbergh, however, had more exciting ambitions. In St. Louis, he obtained backing to bid for a $25,000 prize for the first non-stop Paris-to-New York flight. Lindbergh's silver-painted *Spirit of St. Louis* took off from Long Island, New York on May 20, 1927. Doubters called him the "Flying Fool" for challenging the Atlantic alone. After twenty-four hours flying, only his airplane's movements kept Lindbergh awake. At last, after thirty-three and a half hours, he landed in Paris, reflecting: "I have been to eternity and back." Now known as the

"Lone Eagle," Lindbergh was mobbed in France and England and cheered by millions in a New York ticker tape parade.

Lindbergh's solo flight across the Atlantic, the first ever, was an historic step in aviation, which revived worldwide interest in flying. He made several more record-breaking flights, pioneering the routes for Pan-American's Atlantic-flying passenger airlines.

Always resentful of publicity, Lindbergh found himself in the headlines again when his baby son was kidnapped and murdered in 1932. During World War II (1939–45), Lindbergh was refused an army commission because of his associations with Nazi Germany, but he flew fifty combat missions as a civilian.

After the war, Lindbergh studied German aircraft developments and became an adviser to the U.S. Air Force. He worked in conservation, joined the U.S. space program and became a director of Pan-American Airways before his death in Hawaii in 1974.

Above *Lindbergh stands beside his famous monoplane, the* Spirit of St. Louis.

Below left *When Lindbergh conquered the Atlantic flying solo, he became the most celebrated aviator in history.*

1902	born in Detroit, Michigan
1922	flies barnstorming tours
1927	makes first solo crossing of the Atlantic
1929	marries Anne Morrow
1932	their baby is kidnapped and murdered
1933	makes transatlantic flight with his wife
1934	breaks aviation records in Sikorsky's Clipper airplane
1935	sails to England
1944	flies combat missions in the South Pacific
1974	dies in Maui, Hawaii

14

Amy Johnson

Amy Johnson was one of many people caught up in the flying craze created by Lindbergh's first transatlantic flight. She first flew in a cheap joy-ride at a fair in Hull, England. When she took lessons at the London Aeroplane Club, her instructor told her that she had no flying ability.

However, Johnson got her pilot's license and began working with London's ground engineers. She became the first woman to receive a Ground Engineer's License. Then she began planning a solo flight to Australia.

Johnson took off from Croydon near London on May 5, 1930, in her Gipsy Moth airplane *Jason*. A novice pilot with an amazing sense of direction, but whose landings were haphazard, she battled through sandstorms and monsoon weather. She crash-landed at Insein, Burma, but *Jason* was repaired with war surplus shirts and glue bought from a local drugstore!

"Flying Girl Missing!" the newspapers declared on May 23, but the following day, *Jason*

1903	born in Hull, England
1929	receives her pilot's license; receives Ground Engineer's License
1930	first woman's solo flight England–Australia
1931	record England–Tokyo flight
1932	marries Jim Mollison
1933	flies Atlantic with her husband
1934	Jim and Amy break England–India record
1936	breaks records for England–Cape Town return flight
1941	disappears in the Thames Estuary

Right *Amy Johnson pilots her De Havilland Gipsy Moth airplane* Jason *on one stage of her extraordinary flight from England to Australia.*

landed in Brisbane, Australia. Johnson, as the first woman to fly solo from England to Australia, created a new popular interest in aviation.

She next made the fastest flight from Britain to Tokyo and beat her husband Jim Mollison's record to Cape Town, South Africa. Together, the couple flew the Atlantic, but they crashed in Connecticut, leaving Johnson in poor health.

Jim and Amy broke the record from England to India during a 1934 race to Australia. In 1936, Johnson broke all records for a return flight from England to Cape Town, this time flying alone.

Flying for the Air Transport Auxiliary in World War II, Johnson parachuted into the Thames Estuary during a routine flight on a cold January day in 1941 and was drowned. A mysterious, unidentified passenger was seen with her. Neither body was ever found.

After working tirelessly among London's aircraft mechanics, Johnson became the first woman to receive a British Ground Engineer's License.

15
Frank Whittle

It was only because of a rival cadet's failure to pass his eye test that Frank Whittle was accepted from RAF Apprentice School for officer training at Cranwell College in England. This piece of good fortune transformed aviation history.

At Cranwell, Whittle studied the fighters and bombers that he had watched soar overhead when he was a boy. He learned that, because of the limitations of their piston engines and propellers, no RAF pilot was expected ever to fly faster than 76.2 mph (121.9 kph) or higher than 25,150 feet (7,620 m). Whittle, though, published an essay called "Speculation," proposing an airplane powered by a new type of engine: one which sucked in air, heated it, then expelled it at high speed in a "jet."

After being posted to Central Flying School, Whittle talked to the Air Ministry and several industrial firms, but everyone politely rejected

An RAF Gloster meteor powered by one of Whittle's engines pursues a flying bomb.

his revolutionary ideas. Five years later, a former Cranwell cadet formed a company which was prepared to provide the financial backing that allowed Whittle to build and test successfully the world's first turbojet engine.

The Air Ministry at last provided backing, and at dusk on a bitter day in May, 1941, a test pilot took off from Cranwell in an aircraft fitted with Whittle's engine. This was the secret test flight of Britain's first jet airplane. Research progressed rapidly during World War II. By the summer of 1944, RAF Gloster Meteor jets were fighting Germany's flying bombs, which were also powered by jet engines.

Whittle's engines were used in the American jet industry after the war, and a BOAC (British Overseas Airways Corporation) Comet began the jet age for commercial passengers. Whittle, whose work heralded a new age in aviation, was knighted and became an RAF Air Commodore.

1907	born in Coventry, England
1923	enlists as RAF apprentice
1928	publishes "Speculation" essay
1935	Powerjets Ltd. manufactures Whittle's first jet engine
1941	Britain's first jet airplane flies
1952	BOAC Comet begins jet age for passengers
1989	retired in Britain

16
Jean Batten

Jean Batten was a supreme aviator, whose record-breaking flights pioneered commercial airlines both in her native New Zealand and throughout the world.

She resolved to become an aviator after the great Australian pioneer, Charles Kingsford-Smith, took her on her first flight. It prompted Batten to travel to England's London Aeroplane Club, where she quickly obtained both her private and commercial pilot's licenses.

On May 8, 1934, Jean Batten took off from England in a Gipsy Moth airplane on the first of many historic flights. Despite having to hand-pump fuel from auxiliary to main tanks, she reached Darwin, Australia, in a record fourteen days, twenty-two-and-a-half hours. The following year, she flew back to England to complete the first round-trip flight by a woman.

Below *Jean Batten pilots her Percival Gull over the treacherous Tasman Sea to complete the first direct England-to-New Zealand flight.*

In a new Percival Gull airplane, Batten left England for Brazil, flying high over raging storms to land in Natal, Brazil, after two days, thirteen hours flying. She was the first woman to fly the South Atlantic, and her flight time beat Jim Mollison's England-to-South America record by nearly a day.

In October, 1936, Batten made a record-breaking England-to-Australia flight in under six days. Flying on over the Tasman Sea, she fulfilled her lifelong ambition of making the first direct flight from England to New Zealand, where she received an emotional welcome.

Jean Batten's farewell flight, from Darwin, Australia, to Lympne, England, beat the solo record by fourteen hours. She received her greatest ever reception and became the first woman to receive the medal of the Féderation Aéronautique Internationale, the highest award in aviation.

Batten prepares her Gipsy Moth biplane for her first record-breaking England–Australia flight.

1909	born in Rotorua, New Zealand
1930	receives pilot's license
1934	breaks England–Australia record
1935	completes first woman's England–Australia return flight
1935	first woman's solo South Atlantic crossing
1936	first direct England–New Zealand flight; (Oct.) breaks Australia–England record
1938	receives Medal of the Féderation Aéronautique Internationale
1982	dies in Majorca in the Mediterranean

17

Douglas Bader

One of the most remarkable stories in aviation is that of the British fighter pilot Douglas Bader. An RAF cadet at Cranwell College, Bader was a superb aviator and outstanding sportsman. However, in 1931, his sporting and flying careers were seemingly destroyed when, after his commission as a pilot officer, Bader crashed his aircraft while performing in an aerobatic display. He came close to death, and both his legs had to be amputated.

Within six months, though, Bader was walking again without crutches on artificial legs. He learned to drive a car and became an excellent golfer. A year after the accident, he was flying again, but despite passing his flying tests, Bader was forced to leave the RAF.

At the outbreak of World War II, Bader demonstrated his exceptional flying skills and was allowed to re-enlist. He became a top fighter ace in the Battle of Britain and the London Blitz,

Below *Bader's Hurricane fighter closes for combat with a German Dornier 17Z.*

and was promoted from Squadron Leader to Wing Commander.

In 1941, Bader's plane collided with a German Messerschmitt over occupied France. Only the removal of his artificial right leg permitted him to parachute out. Taken to a prison hospital, he escaped down a rope of knotted sheets before being betrayed to the Germans. Following a second escape attempt, Bader was imprisoned in Colditz Castle, a fortress used by the Germans to hold Allied prisoners of war, until the end of the war.

Back in Britain after the war, Bader continued flying for the Shell Oil company, who had employed him immediately after his first accident. He flew light aircraft throughout the world before making his final flight at the age of sixty-nine. Douglas Bader was knighted in 1976. He died in 1982 at the age of seventy-two. The Douglas Bader Foundation, which he started, continues its research into ways of helping people who have lost one or both legs.

Bader (center) with his RAF comrades.

1910	born in London, England
1931	loses both legs in aerobatic crash
1940	rejoins RAF
1941	promoted to Wing Commander
1941	crashes over France
1941–5	captured by the Germans and held as a prisoner of war
1982	dies in Britain

18

Charles Yeager

Yeager's tiny Bell X-1 Glamorous Glennis *soars away from its B-29 bomber mothership.*

The post-war pioneers of aviation were the test pilots, who risked their lives forcing airplanes to fly ever faster and higher. Perhaps the greatest of them all was Charles "Chuck" Yeager.

Yeager first demonstrated his remarkable flying ability while training as a fighter pilot. Once, he deliberately chopped down a tree with his plane's wing tip. During World War II, he shot down twelve opponents, five in one day, including a German jet fighter.

After the war, Yeager was selected to fly the Bell X-1 airplane through the mysterious "sound barrier" which was believed to exist at the speed of sound. On October 14, 1947, Yeager, nursing two recently broken ribs, clambered down from a B-29 bomber into the orange bullet-shaped X-1 *Glamorous Glennis* which was slung below. The X-1 was released at 20,117 feet (6,096 m). Igniting its rockets,

Yeager climbed into the unknown. At 42,245 feet (12,801.6 m), there was a sonic boom. Yeager hurtled through the invisible sound barrier, becoming the first man to fly a supersonic aircraft.

After his famous flight, Yeager continued to fly revolutionary airplanes to their absolute limit in the greatest era of research flying in aviation history. Many of his contemporaries were killed. Only Yeager's amazing skill as a pilot saved his life when, on one test flight, he set a new speed record of Mach 2.4.

After becoming a successful squadron commander, Yeager was made head of the Air Force Aerospace Research Pilot's School, which trained today's astronauts and space shuttle pilots. He flew 127 combat missions in the Vietnam War (1959–73), before becoming the only American general allowed to pilot aircraft. He retired in 1975 after 10,000 flying hours piloting 180 different military aircraft.

1923	born in Myra, West Virginia
1944–5	flies as fighter pilot over France
1947	flies Bell X-1 through the sound barrier
1953	sets new Mach 2.4 speed record
1954	receives Harmon Trophy
1963	badly burned attempting altitude record
1966	serves in Vietnam War
1968	promoted to general
1973	becomes Safety Director of U.S. Air Force
1975	retires
1976	receives Medal of Honor
1988	living in the U.S.; still flies and challenges new records

19

Dick Rutan and Jeanna Yeager

"Around the world on one tank of gas" was the slogan that accompanied the attempt of Dick Rutan and Jeanna Yeager to circumnavigate the globe without refueling.

Their distinctively-shaped *Voyager* aircraft had been constructed without the support of the government, but with the determination that runs through the whole of aviation history to succeed against all odds.

Voyager, which was designed by Dick's brother Bert Rutan, took two years to complete. It was capable of carrying all the fuel necessary for the non-stop flight. Her wingspan of 111 feet (33.7 m) was nearly as long as the entire first powered flight achieved by the Wright brothers eighty-three years previously!

Rutan and Yeager took off from Edwards Air Force Base, California, on December 14, 1986, and despite suffering damage to *Voyager*, began their epic journey. Since most of the aircraft was one enormous gas tank, the pilot was wedged into a cockpit measuring only 5½×1¾ feet (1.7×.5m). When they were "off duty" they attempted to rest in an impossibly cramped cabin with dimensions of 7½×2 feet (23×.6m).

For nine long days, the two aviators battled through difficult weather, fighting off fatigue and the pressures of living constantly together at such close quarters. At sunrise, December 23, a large crowd welcomed them back to Edwards Air Force Base. *Voyager* touched down after a non-stop flight of 25,160 miles (40,253km) averaging 116.5 mph (186.36 kph). Rutan and Yeager had completed what some considered the ultimate aviation record.

Burt Rutan, Jeanna Yeager and Dick Rutan received presidential Citizen's Medals and plaques from President Reagan in honor of Voyager's *flight.*

Left *Rutan and Yeager pilot* Voyager *over the clouds, in the world's first flight around the world without refueling.*

1938	Dick Rutan born in Loma Linda, California
1952	Jeanna Yeager born in Fort Worth, Texas
1984	work begins on *Voyager* aircraft
1986	Rutan and Yeager complete first circumnavigation without refueling
1988	still flying aircraft in the U.S.; they have written a book about *Voyager*'s flight

20

Bryan Allen

The selection of Californian biologist Bryan Allen to pilot the world's first successful human-powered airplane came about because of his accomplishments not as an aviator, but as a competitive cyclist.

In 1959, British industrialist Henry Kremer offered a prize for the first human-powered aircraft to complete a specified course. To win the prize, an aeronautical engineer, Dr. Paul MacCready, designed the *Gossamer Condor*. Weighing only 70 pounds (31.8 kg), the airplane was made from the lightest possible materials, including corrugated cardboard, piano wire and aluminum tubing. It resembled a huge dragonfly.

The *Condor*'s propeller was turned by bicycle pedals. After a three month training course, Allen was ready to become its "engine." On August 23, 1977, in Shafter, California, Allen – who weighed nearly twice as much as his craft – clambered into the transparent cockpit. Pedaling furiously, he powered the *Gossamer Condor*

1953 born in California
1959 Kremer Prize is offered
1977 Allen achieves first human-powered flight
1979 crosses English Channel in human-powered airplane
1988 still a cyclist, living in the U.S.

gracefully over a course that had defied all previous attempts.

At dawn on June 12, 1979, Allen began an attempted crossing of the English Channel in another human-powered aircraft, the *Gossamer Albatross*. Flying only 10 feet (3 m) above the water, he needed to generate a constant ⅓ horsepower for 22⅗ miles (36.2 km). At the half-way point, *Gossamer Albatross* fell, just inches above the waves. Pedaling desperately up to smoother air, Allen was able to fly on. Fighting a strong headwind and suffering leg cramps and dehydration, he came close to despair. Finally, two hours and forty-nine minutes after take-off, he landed exhausted in France. *Gossamer Albatross*'s fragility was demonstrated when its wing crumpled as the crowd rushed to see it.

Seventy years after Blériot's historic first Channel crossing, Bryan Allen had flown the same distance in an airplane half his weight, powered entirely by his own legs. The dream of generations of aviators – to power a flying machine with their own bodies – had finally come true.

Allen pedals Gossamer Condor *over a course in Shafter, California, and claims the Kremer Prize.*

Below *Bryan Allen pedals furiously to turn the propeller which keeps* Gossamer Condor *airborne.*

Glossary

Ace A top fighter pilot, one who has shot down more than five enemy aircraft.

Aeronautical Related to air navigation.

Aviation The practice of flying an aircraft.

Aviator Someone who flies an aircraft.

Barnstorming Stunt flying to entertain an audience.

Biplane An aircraft with two sets of wings.

Brazier A metal box for burning coal.

Civil engineer A person who designs or makes roads, railroads, bridges, etc.

Civil pilot A non-military pilot.

Dehydration The loss of too much water from the body.

Dirigible A balloon or airship which can be steered.

Dogfight A fight between aircraft.

Emigré Someone who has left his or her native country, often for political reasons.

Glider An airplane with no engine.

Gauges Instruments for measuring wind speed.

Mach The speed of an object in relation to the speed of sound.

Monoplane An aircraft with one set of wings.

Navigable Able to be steered.

Ornithopter An aircraft with flapping wings.

Patent An official document giving one person or firm the sole right to make or sell a new invention.

Reconnaissance aircraft A plane used to find out the position and activities of an enemy.

Sonic boom The noise made when an aircraft goes through the "sound barrier" to fly faster than the speed of sound.

Sound barrier The resistance of the air to objects traveling at the speed of sound.

Supersonic Faster than the speed of sound.

Tethered flight One in which the aircraft is attached to the ground by a long cord.

Triplane An aircraft with three sets of wings.

Wind tunnel An apparatus for producing an air stream, used to test wind resistance on models when designing aircraft.

Further reading

Amelia Earhart – Charles Lindbergh by Naunerle C. Farr & John N. Fago (Pendulum Press, 1979)

Amelia Earhart by Nancy Shore (Chelsea House, 1989)

Barnstormers and Daredevils by K. C. Tessendorf (Macmillan, 1988)

Chuck Yeager, the Man Who Broke the Sound Barrier by Nancy S. Levinson (Walker & Co, 1988)

Famous Aviators of World War II by James B. Sweeney (Franklin Watts, 1987)

Plane Talk: Aviators' and Astronauts' Own Stories by Carl Oliver (Houghton Mifflin, 1980)

Research Airplanes: Testing the Boundaries of Flight by Don Berliner (Lerner Publications, 1988)

Story of Flight, The by Mary L. Settle (Random House, 1967)

Story of the Spirit of St. Louis, The by R. Conrad Stein (Children's Press, 1984)

Wright Brothers at Kitty Hawk, The by Donald J. Sobol (Scholastic Inc., 1987)